Embracing the Journey

*E*mbracing the Journey

AFFIRMATIONS FOR LIVING LIFE
AS A SEXUAL ABUSE SURVIVOR

Nancy W.

HarperSanFrancisco
A Division of HarperCollins*Publishers*

EMBRACING THE JOURNEY: *Affirmations for Living Life as a Sexual Abuse Survivor*. Copyright © 1992 by Nancy W. All rights reserved. Printed in the United States of America. No part of this book may be used or reproduced in any manner whatsoever without written permission except in the case of brief quotations embodied in critical articles and reviews. For information address HarperCollins Publishers, 10 East 53rd Street, New York, NY 10022.

FIRST EDITION

Library of Congress Cataloging-in-Publication Data

W., Nancy.
    Embracing the journey : affirmations for living life as a sexual abuse survivor / Nancy W. — 1st ed.
      p.   cm.
    Includes index.
    ISBN 0–06–250636–6 (alk. paper)
    1. Adult child sexual abuse victims—Rehabilitation.
2. Affirmations. I. Title.
RC569.5.A28W25 1992   91–58141
616.85'83—dc20   CIP

92 93 94 95 96 ❖ COMWEB 10 9 8 7 6 5 4 3 2 1

Contents

Contents

Contents

Acknowledgments

I would like to express my gratitude to the following people:

To all of the women in my Tuesday night group who continue to help me experience hope, healing, laughter, sanity, and a safe place to just *be*. Your insights and courage have been inspirational to me.

To my "regular" listeners and reviewers on this leg of my journey—Lindsey, Lisa D., Lisa R., and Peggy. I appreciated your reactions, suggestions, patience, and encouragement as this book was being created.

To Kathleen, Etta, Charlie, Mary Alice, Jerry, and Sr. Judy for providing a safe and nurturing therapeutic network.

To Barbara Moulton and Barbara Archer at HarperSanFrancisco for their special contributions of time, encouragement, and direction along the way.

To Mari for her help with some of the last minute "fine tuning," and to Caryn for her graciousness and fortitude in reading the *entire* manuscript aloud to me (complete with punctuation!) for the final proofing.

And to all of the people who contributed knowingly or unknowingly to the depth of this book by their presence in my life.

Introduction

Just as my first book, *On the Path*, reflects the unfolding of my recovery process during the year and a half that I spent writing it, so *Embracing the Journey* represents my journey since then. This companion book to *On the Path* includes affirmations about relationships, sexuality, thinking skills, peacefulness, and hope. It focuses less on initial-stage recovery from sexual abuse and more on the challenging issues we face as we embrace and reclaim our lives as survivors. I have discovered that the struggles do not become easier, nor the feelings less intense—just somewhat more manageable. As I work my program of recovery, I find that I experience shorter periods of unmanageability and more moments of serenity and acceptance.

I continue to undergo changes in my beliefs as I heal, and these are reflected throughout the book. My spirituality has probably been the most affected and you may notice that I use the terms Higher Power, higher source, and inner wisdom interchangeably. This is part of my journey.

Introduction

Although there were many more affirmations
that I wanted to write and include, I followed my
usual process of writing about that which was current for me in my healing process. There are many
more pages to be written, and I trust that they will
evolve as I need them. If an affirmation is not in-
cluded that you need, I encourage you to write your
own. I have found writing them to be a wonderful
tool in my recovery. I write affirmations not because
I *fully* believe them now, but because I want and
need to believe them. They emerge from an inner
place of truth and slowly grow into messages of
hope and healing.

This book is intended for use by all survivors—
male and female. I have written it in the first
person female to reflect my own experience. As
in *On the Path*, I support you in editing this book
to suit your own needs. Change pronouns, words,
and ideas so that the text fits for you. The Personal
Index and Notes sections will help you further personalize what is shared here.

I hope that on your journey you will reach out
and enjoy the support that exists for us all. As survivors, we each have unique experiences, but we
have all experienced similar feelings. I believe that
sharing these will be our strength and our path to
further healing.

Embracing the Journey

I Am Growing and Changing

I don't remember when it began or even making a conscious choice to embark on this journey of recovery. I only know that at some point in my life, I began to be acutely aware of some inner stirrings and felt compelled to attend to them. Eventually I began to experience intense feelings that would not be quieted and problems that I could not resolve. I was unhappy, uncomfortable and could not figure out *why* I was feeling this way. I later discovered that the growing unmanageability of my present was directly linked to the abuse in my past.

It has always seemed to me that my process of growth and change has been inevitable—almost without choice. There has always been a voice within me that has urged me to seek to know more about life and myself—to move toward health and wholeness. On my better days, I can now accept that my growth process is a gift bestowed upon me by a higher source. A gift of light, truth, and hope.

Fortunately the changes in the emotional, mental, and spiritual realms of my life have occurred gradually, over time. I probably have not even been aware of the many changes that I have experienced thus far. Some days I may be absolutely certain that no change at all has occurred. Yet there is ample evidence to the contrary. I can get a more accurate picture of how I have changed by reading my old journals, questioning people who have known me for a while and by taking

time to honestly reflect on the differences I can see
and feel in myself. Are some of my wounds less tender
these days? Am I more regularly expressing how I feel?
What I need? Do I more readily make amends? Has
my acceptance of myself and situations increased?
Do I experience serenity more often? Move through
crises more quickly? Am I more present to myself and
others?

Yes, like it or not, I am growing and changing. I
am in the midst of a wonderful and sometimes painful
journey. There is no turning back. There is only
movement forward and a growing trust in the good-
ness of the process.

❀ Today I applaud myself for sticking with my process of healing even when it seems futile or hurts terribly. I can trust that I am moving in exactly the right direction for me.

I Affirm the Courageousness of My Daily Actions

ach action that I take keeps me involved in the forward movement of life. Some days, the most courageous thing I might do is to get out of bed, go to the store, take a shower, or eat. These otherwise ordinary actions can be real triumphs for me when I am in the grip of fear or pain.

There will be days when all the messages I have cataloged in my mind from my abusers will be working against my healing, perhaps even against my living process. These are times when I need to recognize that my "internal offender" is operating and attempting to sabotage my recovery. On these days I will need to muster up every ounce of courage simply to take actions contrary to this life-draining thinking.

I will begin to view each action that I take, no matter how small or what the result, as an act of courage. I will thus be affirming my small but determined survivor spirit.

❀ Today I will focus on my actions rather than my inactions and affirm my inimitable courage to "keep on keeping on."

I Deserve to Be Noticed

I t was safer for me to "blend into the woodwork" when I was a child. I imagined that I could avoid being abused if I wasn't seen. How could anyone hurt me if they couldn't see me? This is how my creative child's mind worked in valiant efforts to try to control the abuse.

Today I may still carry vestiges of this protective behavior. My child-within is often still in a survivor mode. As memories of the sexual abuse continue to surface, I may want to retreat even more into a state of invisibility. This is when my maturing adult-self can reassure that child and allay her fears. That child deserved to be noticed. She deserved to have all her preciousness and uniqueness seen, loved, and cherished by her caregivers. Today *I* can tell her this until she believes it.

There may still be some fear, shame, and a great deal of grief connected with being noticed today. Whenever someone sees the beauty of my spirit or simply notices and appreciates my presence, I may feel waves of sadness. This is the result of the loss of self I suffered long ago. The grieving will be healing and will allow me to gradually see that same spirit or "piece of God" within me that is so apparent to others.

❀ Today I notice myself—that I am alive, thinking, feeling, and acting. I embrace all my feelings about being noticed—by myself and others.

9

I Am Finding My Voice

While growing up, I may sometimes have been described as a "shy" or "bashful" child—perhaps even "backward." My tendency was to become very quiet at times, particularly with new people and in new circumstances. I now recognize this as a creative survivor technique. However, I may have continued to carry this behavior with me into adulthood, often experiencing immense pain due to my seeming inability to express myself verbally—especially in social situations.

I am learning that sexual abuse often robs us of our natural, free-flowing voice. We are working so hard either at a conscious or unconscious level to keep the terrible secrets about the abuse, that talking can often *feel* life-threatening. It may not even feel safe to make sounds as we were often told to keep quiet during the abuse.

In my recovery, I can reclaim my voice by recognizing how I have been expressing myself in other ways—through writing, drawing, movement, music, and other creative endeavors. These are all ways that

I can continue to give "voice" to the old, deep pain
of any abuse that occurred when I was non-verbal. My
survivor-child has created her own mode of expression, and if I can tap into this, I will be able to
be her voice today.

❀ I affirm that today it is safe to make sounds,
talk, and tell all my secrets. My life is no longer
in jeopardy. I can begin very slowly and soon
I will begin to notice the return of my authentic voice. My little one inside has waited so
long to *really* talk. Today I can help her say
all she needs to say in any way that she needs
to say it.

I Am Aware of and Appreciate My Natural Compassion

This day, I accept that I was born naturally compassionate. This very precious attribute was given a negative name by my abusers. I was labeled as "overly sensitive" or "unable to cope with life" instead of being recognized as possessing a beautiful and positive quality. Once again, my abusers managed to steal from me another spiritually life-giving gift.

Today I take time to remember any small acts or thoughts of compassion that I possessed as a child and take time to cherish them. Remembering will help me recognize the feeling of compassion when it occurs in my adult life. I may be aware of this feeling whenever

I observe another living thing being abused. I recognize and can empathize with the feelings of pain that accompany hurtful acts.

I need to be mindful that there is a difference between feeling sorry for or trying to fix someone or some situation, and truly feeling compassion. Compassion is a natural feeling that flows from the heart and leads me down the path of being in touch with my authentic self—the self that is gradually healing and coming out of hiding. Feeling compassion is a connection to the spirit.

❀ Today I notice my compassion—toward others and particularly toward myself. I deserve to feel and acknowledge this lovely gift in my life—a gift that emanates from the innocence of my child-within.

I Can Notice and Appreciate My Senses

Growing up in a threatening abusive atmosphere, I learned very early to use all of my senses to detect danger. I could easily hear noises that others would not notice, see ever so slight movements around me, feel whisper-soft touches on my skin, and smell odors that meant danger was near. Sometimes these abilities enabled me to avoid abuse and other times they afforded me time to "gear up" for the inevitable.

Today as an adult, I sometimes notice that when I hear, see, feel, or smell things and mention my observations to others, they may not be able to affirm these facts for me. This does not mean that my senses are faulty or that I am crazy. It just means that my senses have been trained to be extremely keen.

I can affirm and appreciate my senses today and enjoy them as a very valuable part of me. I no longer have to use them to continue my hyper-vigilance as I once did. I can, however, appreciate that they continue to help me be alert and cognizant of my environment. I can notice how my senses also help me enjoy the beauty and wonder of the world around me. Today there are so many things to hear, see, feel, and smell that will bring joy to my life, and I can be aware of them all.

❀ Today I will not doubt what my senses tell me just because no one else can confirm the data. Instead, I affirm and am grateful that I can use them to notice and enjoy my surroundings.

I Can Make Mistakes and Still Be OK

Being imperfect is not something that is easy for me to admit to today. As a small child, I may have come to the conclusion—albeit mistaken—that if I was only *good* enough, the abuse would miraculously end. I may also have learned from my offender *and* witnesses to the abuse that admitting mistakes was definitely not OK and could be dangerous. It was very important to my offender that I believe he was never wrong. He was highly invested in my believing that any imperfections and inappropriate behaviors were mine, not his.

It is no wonder then, that trying to live a normal, fallible life placed me in a double bind. To admit to my own imperfections would mean that the abuse was my fault, yet achieving perfection was virtually impossible. I was and am, after all, human and fallible. So, the only conclusion my child-mind could reach was that making mistakes was not OK and neither was I.

Today, I am beginning to realize that the feeling of not being OK is called shame and that this shame was passed on to me by my abusers. I am slowly learning to discern how much of the shame I feel belongs to me and how much of it belongs to my offenders. As I am able to return shame that is not mine and admit to my own, I become more accepting of myself as a fallible human being. Forgiving myself for making mistakes and affirming that I am still OK places me on the road to self-acceptance and healing.

❀ This day, I accept my humanness—complete with fallibility—and rejoice in the freedom this belief offers me.

I Accept and Affirm
My Present Sense of Knowing

I may often wonder why sometimes I can accept that I was sexually abused and other times, I *truly* believe that it never happened to me. There are and will be days when I feel that my recovery process is no more than a hoax—based on lies, misperceptions, and exaggerations. Since I do not *know* or remember the abuse with a sense of certainty, I believe that I am just using this issue as a means to get attention, fit in, or explain my poor self-esteem and other "defective" qualities.

When I am thinking and feeling this way, I will endeavor to accept myself as coming from a place of truth. Just for today, I need to believe these things. It is part of my process—my journey. Rather than fighting these perceptions, I may find that embracing them will calm my internal storms.

During these times it may be helpful to realize that I may never experience a sense of full cognitive knowing or memory, particularly if abuse occurred during early childhood. I will only have as much knowledge and memory as my child could developmentally understand, process, and *allow in* at the time. My truth will consist of whatever fragments it is safe for me to remember and "know" on any given day. I will reverence this knowing and not allow anyone— including myself—to try to force it to be otherwise.

❀ Today I accept my truth—my sense of knowing—exactly as it is right now.

I Can Use Protective Behaviors Whenever I Need to Slow Down My Healing Process

Healing from childhood sexual abuse can be a long and arduous process. I may find that I advance in spurts, according to how much reality I can handle at a time. When I encounter a particularly difficult and perhaps even overwhelming truth about my abuse, I may need to slow down considerably, even come to a halt, in my active process of recovery (feeling my feelings, remembering, and so on).

It is during these times of intense vulnerability that I can give myself permission to use any protective behaviors that I need in order to maintain my sanity and stay alive. As a child, I may not have been able to acknowledge the reality of the abuse *and* stay alive. Today I may recycle that same thought and accompanying feelings of fear and panic. I truly believe that I will die if I continue to pursue the truth about my abuse. This is my child-within speaking to me and entreating me to be gentle with her precious being.

I can acknowledge that using old survivor behaviors like spending the day in bed, reading, watching television, going on "automatic pilot," doing mundane things, or even denying the abuse momentarily can help me make it through what I believe to be potentially life-threatening periods of recovery. Using these behaviors does not mean that I will ignore the truth forever but rather that I am treating my child-within with respect and listening to her needs. I can always resume my *active* healing process when we both feel safe again. I believe it is acceptable to be in "neutral" for as long as necessary.

❀ Today I will honor my own unique healing
process by doing and believing whatever I need
to in order to continue to survive. Surviving is
the first step in recovery.

When I Am Unable to Trust,
I Can Act on Blind Faith

T here have been and will be many times in
my life when I simply am not able to
trust—myself, a Higher Power, or other
people. As a survivor of childhood sexual abuse, my
ability to trust was thwarted at an early age and has always been minimal, at best.

I may be frustrated at times when to trust would
mean to reach out, take a risk, and grow. I may in fact
want desperately to trust but cannot. It is at these
times that I can act on blind faith instead. Acting on
blind faith does not require trusting. It only asks that I
act "as if"—that I give myself permission to try something even though I still may question its validity or
helpfulness.

"Faith isn't faith until it's all you're hanging on

to" is a popular saying nowadays. This adage helps me remember that the life-spark in my child-within has always possessed some form of faith, no matter how minute. Otherwise I would not be here today seeking recovery. I can acknowledge this carefully preserved nugget of faith and act on it whenever I cannot trust. It will carry me through times when instead of "figuring things out," I need to simply act.

❀ When I find it impossible to trust, I will be gentle with myself and remember that I can act on blind faith—again. That is how I can continue to move forward on my path of recovery in spite of what appears to be a possible roadblock.

I Acknowledge and Affirm My Natural Sexual Feelings

The word *sex* can conjure up a myriad of thoughts, feelings, and memories for me—many of which may be confusing and frightening. What I have lacked, as a sexual abuse survivor, is a connection with and knowledge of my *natural* sexual feelings. These are the feelings that everyone is born with and that are a beautiful and normal part of being human.

I may have learned to shame myself for feeling sexual. My abusers may even have told me that I was being violated by them because *I* wanted sex. How confusing for me as a child to be feeling sexual, ashamed, and terrified all at the same time. Today I may find that I feel sexually stimulated when I hear or think about violent sexual acts. This is because my natural sexual feelings were first linked with violence. I will have compassion for myself when this occurs and affirm that this is a normal reaction for me as a survivor.

When I feel sexual today, I may continue to re-play the offender's messages in my head. This can prevent me from celebrating and enjoying a most important and precious part of myself. Instead, I can allow myself to feel sexual, knowing that I have the power to choose when and if I will act on that feeling. This will create a safe space within me to continue to affirm and develop a healthy sexuality.

Feeling sexual is a gift that will blossom as I affirm its naturalness and beauty. I will begin to discover that I feel sexual in response to a variety of stimuli. I can enjoy them all, knowing that I am birthing a vibrant and long dormant part of me.

❀ Today I will celebrate any sexual feelings I
might experience and affirm their normalcy.
I deserve to feel sexual—free of fear or shame.
I reclaim the beauty of my human sexuality
for myself and my child-within.

I Am Capable of Having Mutually Honest and Loving Relationships

I may have noticed that many of my relationships have been one-sided and reminiscent of relationships I had with one or both of my parents. Whether romantic or platonic, my present-day relationships may continue to cause me deep pain and confusion and often leave me feeling inept, hopeless, and lonely—particularly when change or conflict occurs.

As a survivor of sexual abuse, I may still be looking to others for the loving connectedness I never experienced as a child. I may demand of friends and lovers more than they can ever give me and this will often cause me to see myself as a failure in relationships. If I acknowledge that my childhood experiences of relating to others were terrifying, unhealthy, and isolating, I can begin to accept my intimacy skills exactly as they are—in process.

I can see each person I have been or am presently in a relationship with as a teacher. Each one will help me to see areas where I need to change and heal. For this I can be grateful and acknowledge my courage for not giving up.

I will be caring and kind to my adult-self and particularly to my child-within as we heal in this area. I will continue to affirm that I deserve and am most capable of engaging in mutually satisfying relationships. I will feel and express my pain and anger about my early losses, thus opening pathways to ever maturing relationships—with myself and others.

❀ Today I take time to recognize my innate capabilities to love and be honest. These qualities will enable me to engage in relationships that are safe, healthy, and satisfying.

I Am Learning to Trust My Ability to Think

Although I may have survived by my wits, my thinking has always seemed somewhat confused and at times overwhelming. Since I may have been labeled as "crazy" by my offenders and told that I was making up events that seemed real to me, even *I* began to question my thinking skills—perhaps my sanity.

Sexual abuse naturally creates disturbing thoughts that are often connected to powerful feelings. Today I may find that my thinking becomes clearer as I am able to embrace my feelings. I may notice that violent thoughts dissipate when I can acknowledge and express my anger; that thoughts of hopelessness will wane when I can feel my pain and sadness; and that some thoughts are just that— thoughts. My brain is constantly active so I will always be thinking. As I become more comfortable with myself and my feelings, I can begin to be more accepting of all my thoughts. I no longer have to be afraid of my own mind. The insanity of the incest does not belong to me.

I can begin today to affirm my innate capability to think things through, to make decisions and to solve problems. These abilities may have saved my life in the past and I can thank this part of me for the protection it provided. I can use these same skills in the present, less as a defense and more as a support for my healing process. I can have confidence in my own thinking as I let go of old distorted thought patterns and lies connected to my abuse. My thinking can, in combination with the physical, emotional, and spiritual parts of me, work for my greatest good in recovery.

❀ Today I affirm my ability to think, and trust that how and what I think is getting clearer all the time.

I Can Walk Through My Fear

F ear is as familiar to me as breathing. At times it manifests itself as anxiety and can easily escalate into panic or even paralyzing terror. It is a feeling I have had as long as I can remember and one I seem to experience on a daily basis. At times it has been so intense and constant that I believed I would never survive another moment of it. It truly can take on a life of its own.

All children need to develop a healthy fear of dangerous things. This is how they learn to make wise decisions about their safety. However, as an incest survivor, I was subjected early on to terrorizing experiences that cast away any chance I might have had to see fear as an ally.

In recovery, I have discovered that I can walk through any feelings of fear that arise. I can begin by breathing, getting grounded in the present, and by creating a sense of safety around me. Next, I can assure myself that I *can* stand the feeling. I may choose to express it and even share it with someone, if that feels safe. I don't have to know what's causing the fear. That may come later. I may be surprised to find that enormous amounts of pain and anger underlie the terror and anxiety. All these feelings were frozen within my child, and today I can help her at last give expression to them.

Fear no longer has to be crippling or rob me of my inner freedom. Each time that I feel my fear and move through it, I am diffusing the power of the offender. I am saying that I will no longer be controlled by my abuse. I will feel the fear and take action in spite of it! My child-within no longer needs to carry old terror. I can help her release it so that we can both live in the present.

❀ Each time that I feel fear, I will own it, feel
as much as I can, and then do whatever is
necessary to walk through it. I will affirm
my courage and my commitment to life as I
do this.

I Am in the Process of Reclaiming Myself

To reclaim means to seek the restoration or return of something. The longer I am engaged in recovery from sexual abuse, the clearer it becomes that I am in the process of reclaiming my original and authentic self—the self that has been buried under layers of shame, terror, pain, and lies. I will find that the roots of this self reside in my life spark and the indomitable spirit of my child-within. No matter how brutal the abuse, my sense of self is only hidden—*not* non-existent, as I have sometimes feared.

The very nature of sexual abuse causes an intense

blurring of boundaries and a temporary loss of self for the victim. It is not surprising then that I have consistently found myself involved in enmeshed relationships—never knowing where I begin and end or who I am apart from someone else. I may find that I frequently define what I believe I should do, think, or feel by comparing myself to others. Part of my restoration will be to begin to detach myself from entangled relationships where I seem to lose my sense of self. I will instead begin to focus on what *I* want, feel, and think.

As I do this, I will feel the return of something

akin to a joy in being alive—in simply being *me*. This is my self re-emerging and basking in the light of life. I will begin to enjoy my own company and find that my frantic need to be emotionally attached to another person will gradually diminish. I will be in the active and exciting process of finding me. And I will begin to feel more centered, content, and trusting of myself.

❀ Today I can celebrate the gradual return of my
sense of self and feel the joy in being the me I
was always meant to be.

I Can Question the Existence of a Higher Power and Still Feel Safe

There may be numerous times during my recovery when I am completely unable to trust or believe in any type of "Higher Power." I may feel confused or frightened about this, especially if I have looked to a Higher Power for strength, hope, and support in the past.

It is comforting to allow myself to question the existence of a Higher Power *and* still believe that I am safe and most healable. Sometimes just affirming myself with this type of statement will be enough to carry me through the difficult times.

Believing in a Higher Power will probably ebb and flow for me during my recovery process. After all, the sexual abuse stripped me of my natural sense of spirituality and I am slowly rebuilding beliefs and trust in this area. As I discover new memories and feelings, my faith and trust in *anything* will be pushed to the limit. It is especially during these times that I can be gentle with and accepting of myself and my child-within. I will support my own beliefs—whatever they are—and know that I am actively in the process of healing.

❀ Today I can question, have doubts, and still feel safe as I mend from the effects of my sexual abuse.

I Am Learning to Accept the Unique Form and Timing of My Memories

As I continue in my recovery from sexual abuse, I may find that my memories will present themselves in many forms. They may come to me through dreams, drawing, writing, meditation, daydreaming, overwhelming feelings, and many other unexpected avenues. My natural inclination may be to discount any memories that do not surface in my conscious awareness. I may tell myself that if I don't *truly* remember the events, they didn't happen.

If I can recognize and accept this reaction as one

of my most important survival skills exercising itself,
I will be able to see beyond it to the messages I am
receiving from my unconscious. This may be difficult
at first and perhaps even frightening. My need for
control will be great. But I can begin to let go and
entertain the validity of these memories gradually—
at my own pace.

Memories may come at what I consider to be
most inopportune times and perhaps before I feel
ready for more data. Once again, if I can simply
acknowledge the information that is being presented

to me, my acceptance and belief in it can occur over time.

My offenders programmed me to disbelieve myself, to mistrust my perceptions, and to doubt my thinking skills. This is how they ensured protection from their atrocious crimes. My memories are my child-within's courageous way of exposing the truth. Today I can honor her by beginning to acknowledge her messages.

❀ I am becoming willing to acknowledge that
my memories may come through unexpected
channels and at unplanned times. I will allow
my acceptance of the data to unfold at a safe
pace for me.

I Am Willing to Examine My Beliefs and Feelings about Sexual Relationships

Although I may have engaged in sexual relationships in the past, they very often left me unsatisfied, frightened, and confused. I may even have attempted to use sex as a way to feel that I mattered—but again with disappointing results. If ever the devastating effects of my sexual abuse were apparent, it was during these situations.

With the clearest intentions of fostering a healthy sexual relationship with someone, I may have found myself desperately lonely during or particularly after having sex. I may have noticed that I could hardly bear to have that person leave me and that I felt incredibly lonely and rejected when he or she did. What is a normal chain of events in separating after

intimacy, felt like a life-or-death situation to me. I
found myself terrified of having that person leave me,
even briefly.

If I can look at these feelings and beliefs in light
of my sexual abuse, I can see how they all make
perfect sense. As a child, I was used sexually and then
abandoned—perhaps even threatened. When no one
came to my aid or even to comfort me, I learned that
I was truly alone. I also mistakenly surmised that this
was the way sex was supposed to feel. It may have
been my only way of being recognized and what I
assumed was mattering to someone else.

❖ Today I need to be most loving and gentle with
my precious child-within who still has skewed
views of sexual relationships. I need to help her
feel her mattering in self-loving ways so that I
can be free to explore my adult sexual relationships in a safe, caring, and mutually health-
giving manner.

I Recognize and Have Patience with My Longing for a Healthy Sexual Relationship

As I watch other couples—in real life, on television, or in the movies—engage in romantic and sexual relationships, I may be aware of envy and a deep longing within myself. I feel a longing for closeness—physical and emotional. A longing to be touched gently and sensually and to experience my own sexual yearnings and pleasures. I may find that even simply talking about a sexual relationship may tap into this deep feeling.

In an effort to fulfill this sense of longing, I may engage in obsessive fantasy or even stay connected to a long dead or unhealthy relationship—particularly in my thoughts. I want so badly to experience intimacy both physically and emotionally that I will go to any lengths.

If I am willing to recognize and have patience with this intense and long-awaited desire, I will actually be creating space for my child-within to heal. My longing is most understandable and normal. After all, the sexual abuse taught me only negative and unhealthy ideas about sexual relationships. My child-within and I deserve the time to heal and learn new beliefs. I may experience grief and loneliness as I own my past and present realities. These feelings can be a crucial part of my healing process if I will fully acknowledge and experience them.

❀ I can affirm that I deserve to have a healthy sexual relationship if I choose to and that it has more of a chance to evolve if I first attend to my inner healing. My wounded child-within needs my attention first and foremost. I affirm my ability to be patient, experience my feelings, *and* to have my longing simultaneously.

My Nighttime Dreams Are Part of My Healing Process

As I am recovering from the sexual abuse, I may experience nightly dreaming that is often disturbing, puzzling, and even surrealistic. Things don't seem to make sense and I may feel frightened by some of the images or scenarios that occur in my dreams. I may feel afraid to go to sleep at times because it is during sleep that my conscious state takes a rest and my unconscious goes into gear. Having a strong need to control (as a result of the abuse), sleeping may at times be an unwelcome event.

If I can begin to simply accept that I will experience dreams—sometimes disturbing—I will be allowing my unconscious an opportunity to express what my conscious self is unable to say, feel, or think. I can receive healing through my dreaming as I allow my whole self—conscious and unconscious—to express itself. I will receive many gifts through this process. I need only accept it as a normal part of my recovery from the sexual abuse. I can endure the unpleasant feelings surrounding sleep and dreams by affirming that this is a much-needed part of my healing process and by knowing that other survivors are experiencing and growing from similar circumstances.

❀ Today I will simply accept my dreams as friends that are helping me heal through expression of my feelings and thoughts.

I Am Learning to Let Go of Jealousy

I may constantly compare myself—my physical appearance, my intellect, and even my actions—to other people. I may particularly compare my physical attributes to people of the same sex—always finding myself lacking.

This behavior may always be with me but I can lessen its effects by acknowledging the roots of its cause—shame. My sexual abuse set me up to believe that I was shameful, ugly, less than, and generally not acceptable. I need to be clear today that this shame is not mine. It belongs to my abuser. When I was sexually abused, I lost sight of my innate preciousness and beauty, and the induced shame caused me to always be seeking to be "better."

Today I can notice when feelings of jealousy begin to form and acknowledge their source. It may be helpful to visualize returning the shame to my abusers and affirm my present uniqueness and beauty verbally or otherwise.

Perhaps I will never be as talented, attractive, or intelligent as I'd like to be, but if I continue to compare myself to others out of jealousy, I will miss the real me. I can begin to slowly let go of my feelings of jealousy by acknowledging them, knowing that they are "normal" for me, and by taking time to embrace my inherent worth, just as I am. I was created to be me—nobody else—and that is a precious gift.

> When I notice that I am feeling jealous, I will acknowledge this feeling, own it, and let go of any shame connected to it. I will affirm that I am enough just as I am.

I Am Willing to Know My Truth

My feelings about the truth have varied widely throughout my life. I may have done all I could at times to avoid looking at it, while at other times I sought it out with a vengeance. Not consciously *knowing* the truth has been one of my most important survivor skills, and today I can be truly grateful for its existence. If I want to continue to heal from my sexual abuse I need to, at some point, become willing to know whatever truth is retrievable. I can go as slowly as I need to with this process. I need only have the willingness to begin.

The truth with which I am most familiar was told

to me by my offenders. Today I know that this is *most* distorted and is probably the *least* trustworthy. My truth can only come from within me. No one else can tell me what it is. Even if someone else affirms what I believe to be true, I am the one who ultimately has to decide if I will accept and embrace it as my truth.

My truth will emerge from many parts of me. I have been conditioned to believe that I will only know the truth through my capacity to think. However, since parts of the truth cannot be recovered through conscious remembering or surmising alone, I will need to trust other facets of my self to supply the missing pieces. My feelings and body contain much valuable information if I am willing to listen to and trust what they have to say. Since I was basically taught to mistrust and disregard these parts of my self, I will need to be willing to put aside old perceptions and risk learning a new way of knowing. As I am able to do this, I will receive the gift of at last being able to trust myself. I will no longer need anyone to tell me what *my* truth is. I will know.

❀ Today I will slowly begin to listen to what my feelings and body are telling me. Together with my thinking, this is how I will come to know and trust my truth.

I Deserve As Much Privacy As I Need

My right to privacy is something I am just beginning to understand and claim. As a child, I always sensed when my privacy was being violated by some signal or feeling in my body. My mind may not even have consciously registered the thought. But my body knew.

If by chance I did recognize the lack of privacy in my home, I may have attempted to protect myself in creative ways, to control other people's actions by clever manipulation or I may simply have "spaced out" whenever my privacy was violated. I came to view intrusion as acceptable and "normal" behavior.

Today I know that I no longer have to tolerate any intrusion of my personal space, *especially* the subtle sexual abuse that often accompanies this violation.

I can state my needs to others and if these requests are not respected, I can take adult action to protect myself and gain the privacy I deserve. Today I accept no excuses or justifications.

Some people may tell me that I am "overreacting" or am "too sensitive" about my need for privacy. I know differently. I know the truth. I deserve every bit of privacy that I need, no matter where or when. I am no longer a small, unprotected person. I am an adult who can name it and claim it!

❀ I will continue to gain the trust of my child-within by taking action in the present to obtain my richly deserved privacy and will honor and express any feelings that arise when it is violated.

I Can Stand Up for What I Believe

I may find my beliefs being constantly challenged by others and perhaps even by myself. It has been difficult to really trust my reality or beliefs because I have experienced so much discounting of my truths throughout my life. I may have been told that the sexual abuse did not occur and that I was "making it all up." In order to hold on to some sense of security, I may have chosen to deny my truth in order to belong or even survive.

As I continue to commit myself to recovery from the abuse, I may experience periods of confusion when I am truly unsure of my own truth or beliefs. However, there is a knowing voice inside of me that can tell me when to question someone else's statements about me or behavior toward me. If I listen to this voice and take action—no matter how scared I feel—I can discover and affirm my truth and source of strength within.

The most important thing is not to take on someone else's truth as my own but rather to have the courage to believe myself first and foremost. My child-within needs desperately to know that I will believe and champion her—no matter what. This will be my act of courage—to stand up for what I believe—even when I am most afraid. No one stood up for me as a child. Now I can do this for myself.

✿ Today I will listen to the voice of truth within me and affirm it with some small action. I can even get support as I do this. Each time that I take action on my behalf, I will be moving toward trusting and believing in myself.

I Can Allow Myself to Be Held and Comforted by Safe People

Perhaps one of the things that I, as an incest survivor, crave more than anything else, is to be held and comforted in a loving and safe way. Finding someone to do that for me as a child was probably an impossible task. The non-sexual holding or comforting I received was most often perfunctory—such as when I was physically hurt or ill.

What I really longed for and deserved was to be cuddled and loved by my caregivers just because I was me. I may have desperately wanted to crawl up on my mother's or father's lap to be held and comforted so

that I could at last believe that the world was really
a safe and nurturing place.

Instead, my sexual abuse taught me that physical
closeness most often meant fear, pain, and loneliness.
Touch may have become a fearful or hollow experience at best. Yet there was a part of me that still se-
cretly longed to be lovingly held more than anything
else I could imagine.

Today I affirm that I deserve to be held and comforted in a gentle and non-sexual way. I can use my
adult judgment and the wisdom of my child-within to

choose safe people with whom to experience this. I can begin with very small increments of time and most importantly, I can be in charge of how, where, and how long I want the experience to last. I may choose to be held during times when I am hurting emotionally or simply to experience how it feels to be held in a non-sexual way. Little by little, I will see how I can allow myself to experience being held more often, trusting myself to safely and lovingly orchestrate the process.

❀ Today I give myself permission to begin to experience a long-sought-after dream. When I am ready, I will allow myself to be held, if only for one second, by someone who feels safe to me. I will acknowledge how this feels and congratulate myself on my courage and commitment to my process of healing from my sexual abuse.

I Can Begin to Gently Let Go of Unfulfilled Dreams

There may be many dreams that I have carried close to my heart for a very long time. Year after year, I patiently searched for some ray of hope that indicated one of them might come true. And time after time, I was disappointed and disillusioned. I may have wondered why my desires were going unfulfilled while other people were receiving what I longed for so desperately. What was wrong with me? Why was I being passed over? How much longer could I wait?

I may have deduced that I was somehow undeserving of receiving what I wished for. I may even have surmised that something or someone was punishing me. Depression and despair fed my already low self-esteem. I felt truly defective and unworthy.

Today I can begin to recognize that some of my dreams will be unfulfilled but not because I am unworthy or lacking. Rather, I carry with me a legacy of sexual abuse that has stunted my growth in many areas. My history has robbed me of the fulfillment of some of my fondest dreams and I deserve to have *all* of my feelings about these losses.

As I am able to grieve the losses of some dreams that are truly past fulfillment, I can begin to slowly and gently release them. Having my feelings will be my path to freedom and acceptance and, at last, a sense of serenity. As I do this, I will be making space for new dreams and wishes.

❀ Today I can begin to recognize and accept that some of my life's dreams will go unfulfilled. I will be kind and loving to myself as I do this, always affirming that I am most worthy.

I Am Willing to Let Go of My Role As the "Flawed" Child

I may have grown up believing there was something terribly wrong with me. I saw myself as defective, lacking whatever it took to really *live* my life. I spent years just getting by, just surviving life. Outwardly I may have appeared to be all together while inside I carried the deep-seated belief that I would *never* be a whole person.

As a survivor of incest, I now recognize all the ways my role as a flawed child was supported by my perpetrators. If I could be identified as the "problem," then the truth could be averted. The more attention I received for my defectiveness, the easier it was to deny the sexual abuse. I may have been taken to doctors, psychologists, or other helping professionals in an effort to get me "fixed." Or perhaps I was simply

referred to as the "problem child"—directly or indi-
rectly. Since, as a child, I believed and trusted the
judgment of my caretakers, it was natural for me to
assume that they were telling me the truth. Once
again, I was betrayed *and* re-victimized.

Today, I can feel my feelings about the lies that
were told to me and the way my very essence was
used to keep the secret about the abuse. I can acknowledge that my feelings of defectiveness stem
from a role given to me by my abusers—not from any
inherent flaws in my character or being.

❀ I affirm that I am and always have been whole
   and complete. As I slowly recover, I will come
   to truly *know* this on a deep level and I will discover the *real* me.

I Recognize and Honor My Desire to Feel Connected

Sexual abuse created a sense of isolation and aloneness in me that no person or thing could seem to touch. It was during those moments of violation that the "hole in my soul" was born. I was plummeted into a dark place within myself that could receive no visitors. I felt totally disconnected from my world and perhaps even myself.

To heal this part of myself will be perhaps one of my greatest challenges. I am so well acquainted with feeling totally isolated that connecting may be extremely frightening and threatening at first. Yet, if

I look to the life spark of my innocent child-within,
I will become acutely aware of my natural human
need and desire to feel lovingly connected—to myself, to others, to my world, and to a spiritual source.

My sense of connectedness will develop as I
am willing to acknowledge, re-experience, and walk
through old feelings of isolation and loneliness. I may
find that I feel most isolated when I am repressing
some feeling that I still find "unacceptable." Owning
and expressing my honest feelings will create a trusting bond with myself and my child-within.

I will also need to be willing to reach out to others and my outer world—especially when I am feeling most alone. I don't have to *feel* a connection— I just have to make it. Over time the feeling will evolve naturally. By giving a voice to my needs and taking action, I will be defeating my offender's original intent of keeping me isolated and mute. I will affirm as often as needed that I am most capable and deserving of being connected in a healthy and life-supporting way.

❀ I have been alone too long. Today I will take some small step to connect with myself and my world and affirm my courage in doing so.

I Deserve to Have My Possessions Respected

Although I may be striving to lessen the importance of material things in my life, there is still an angry and hurt child within me who needs to heal from having not only her being but her personal and precious possessions disrespected as well.

Having grown up in a family where there were few or no boundaries, my child-within may have clung to some very special possessions as things that she could at least attempt to protect from abuse. This may have given her the much needed feeling of having some control over her self and her environment.

Today, when my possessions are treated with disrespect, I may experience powerful feelings of anger and sadness. These feelings are a carry-over from having experienced similar invasive situations as a child. Lacking the knowledge that these feelings— especially the anger—were healthy and appropriate, I had to push them deep down inside of me.

This day I will affirm that all of my possessions, large or small, animate or inanimate, tangible or intangible, deserve to be treated with respect. I can set boundaries around my possessions and follow through with actions if people ignore these boundaries. I will allow my child-within all her feelings about this issue and not try to "should" her into forgiveness or try to minimize her feelings. She may need to grieve the enormous loss of respect in her life and I will support her in doing this.

❀ Today I claim my right to have myself and all that belongs to me treated with respect. I will honor all my feelings about this issue, thus allowing my child-within to heal and to begin to trust my adult self.

I Can Bloom Where I'm Planted

I may have spent a major portion of my life searching for just the right person, time, or place to *really* begin my life and be truly happy. Looking for perfect conditions today is a direct result of my childhood belief that the sexual abuse would end once I found this magical place. In this utopia, I believed that all the horror, terror, and pain would disappear and I would finally feel content and "normal."

As I continue in my recovery, I am slowly coming to realize that there is no perfect place or person that will "cure" all my troubles. I can, however, honor the resourceful child in me that created this make-believe refuge of hope. This image helped me to survive the horrible reality of the abuse.

Today I recognize that I can finally end my
search. I need only look inside myself to begin to find
the peace and serenity I so richly deserve and have
waited for so steadfastly. Being exactly where I am
and who I am at any given moment is not an easy
task, but one that will eventually engender hope and
healing. As I learn to love and accept each part of
myself, I will find that I can in fact "bloom where I
am planted." I need seek out no more geographical
cures. I need not wait one more day or minute. I can
begin my process of healing right now. I can put my
roots down in the soil of my own being.

❀ **Wherever I am today, I will notice my surroundings *and* my inner self and affirm that
I can grow right where I am. The search is
over. I have arrived.**

I Am Willing to Believe the Unbelievable

One of the ways I can enhance my process of healing from sexual abuse is to be willing to believe the unbelievable. My child-within may be sending me important messages. Unless I am open to acknowledging the totally unfathomable, I may miss significant recovery opportunities.

My initial reaction to this idea may be one of fear and rejection. The memories I do have may already seem overwhelming. To consider even more bizarre and painful occurrences may seem to be too much to ask of my fragile psyche.

However, if I can simply be open to possibilities, I may find that I will receive valuable information that in time will be crucial to my healing process. New data can provide much needed "puzzle pieces"

or explain my often unexplainable feelings or
reactions.

It will be a courageous act on my part to be willing to attend to thoughts that seem terrifying, grue-
some, and totally unacceptable. I will recognize and
respect my child-within's fortitude in moving toward
truth and wholeness. I don't have to believe anything
until I feel ready and unless it feels true for me. I can
engage in this process gradually and accept much-
deserved support along the way.

❀ Today I am willing to "try on" new ideas even
   when they seem totally unthinkable to me. I
   can then gradually decide to keep what fits and
   discard the rest. I will thus be honoring my
   child-within's heroic attempts to communicate
   with me.

I Deserve to Be Treated With Respect and Dignity

I may be so used to being abused that it has become a familiar and accepted way of life for me. Through the acts of my abusers, I was taught that I deserved the treatment I received and that served to feed my already low self-esteem. When I was sexually abused, I was stripped of any expectations that I deserved respect and possessed any dignity.

Today, as an adult, I can recognize that I deserve to be treated with respect and dignity at all times. Regardless of my history or even present behavior, I still deserve to be seen and treated as a human being with worth—just because I am alive.

As I recover, I will become more aware of times when I have been abused by someone else's words, actions, or inactions. With this growing awareness, I can affirm my own worth and choose how I want to handle situations where I have once again been violated or abused. The most important thing for me is to *believe* that I deserve to be treated with respect and dignity. Believing will be my impetus to act in ways that are respectful and supportive of my self.

❀ Today I will appreciate and support my rights to respectful and dignified treatment from others *and* myself.

I Can Be Patient With My Need to Feel a Spiritual Connectedness

My quest for a loving God or spiritual source has been a long and sometimes discouraging journey for me. There have been and will be many times in my life when any feeling of spiritual connectedness completely eludes me. In fact, I may find that my experiences of feeling spiritually "in tune" are sporadic and fleeting. This reality can be dismaying if I have always believed that once I finally felt this spiritual connectedness, it would last forever. It can be reassuring to talk to other people—especially other survivors—and find that my reality is quite normal. I will discover that I am not alone. This knowledge can help me remain patient and trusting during spiritually barren periods.

My child-within may be disappointed, angry, and perhaps even frightened by this process. After all, she was robbed of a natural spiritual connection to herself and her world by the sexual abuse and she may have lost faith in the value of patience. Her childlike hope and yearning for a feeling of spirituality may have turned into skepticism and despair. She will need special reassurance about the existence of a loving spiritual source that is available to her *and* within her.

When I feel most out of touch spiritually, I can continue to invite the feeling of connectedness into my life. I can do this by exploring and discovering ways that I spiritually connect to life. It may be through nature, music, art, meditation, body movement, expression of feelings, or simply taking in the essence of life through all of my senses.

❀ I affirm my natural right to feel a spiritual
connectedness to myself, my world, and
a loving spiritual source. Today I will find
one way to nurture my own precious spirit
while trusting that the feeling of connectedness will once again return.

I Am Learning to Listen to and Respect My Body's Signals

My body is very wise and can provide me with important information if I will only listen to it. As a sexual abuse survivor, I may have become used to tuning out my body and disregarding distress or physical pain. I treated physical symptoms only when they became unbearable. Or, I may have gone to the other extreme, worrying about any pain or change in my body and going to any lengths to "fix" the imperfection. In either case, I probably did not connect any of this distress with emotional needs or body memories.

In recovery, I can begin to acknowledge that my body is a wonderful barometer for what is happening to me on a physical, emotional, and spiritual level. When one of these areas is in need of attention, my body will give me a signal. Perhaps I may experience some sort of body ache, gastrointestinal distress, a general soreness, or fatigue—to name a few. Whatever the message is, my body will attempt to convey it to me. All I need do is listen. Perhaps the best I can do on some days is simply to treat the physical symptoms until any emotional underpinnings become apparent.

As I get healthier, I will notice that I am listening more frequently to my body and attending to the messages I am receiving. I will begin to rest when I need to, eat when I am hungry, exercise for fun, and work through any pain or emotional distress I might experience. I will thus be reclaiming my body and integrating it into the being that is me.

❀ Today I will take time to pay attention to how my body feels and thank my body for its wisdom. It is helping me heal and become whole.

93

I Can Doubt the Occurrence of My Sexual Abuse and Still Be in Recovery

Denial of my sexual abuse is what kept me alive as a child. I may have denied my feelings, my memories, or both. I needed to believe that *someone* was trustworthy and protecting me. I was even willing to question my own reality in order to believe I was being cared for.

As I recover from my sexual abuse, the reality of the heinous acts may again become too much for me to comprehend. It is during these times that I may find myself doubting the occurrence of the sexual abuse. I may also move into denial in order to support my own belief that I am, in fact, *not crazy*. Accepting that I was abused when members of my family deny this fact can cause me to feel crazy and believe once again that "I made it up." Those four familiar words can resurface at any time in my recovery when I feel overwhelmed or threatened.

Whatever my reasons for questioning the reality of my abuse, I can be most gentle with myself and acknowledge that no matter what I believe, I am actively in the process of recovery. Denial is a normal part of my ongoing process of healing and will recycle itself as many times as I need it. I will not shame myself for using this survivor skill. Instead, I will reach out to other survivors who understand for support and affirmation.

❀ Today I accept the paradox that I can doubt or deny the occurrence of my abuse and still be in recovery. Recovery is cyclical, and I will move through each cycle and all its stages as I am ready.

I Deserve to Feel a Sense of Peace

Throughout the turmoil and insanity of my abuse, peace became the dream of a place where I would one day arrive—a place where chaos and intrusion would end, and tranquility would prevail. I continued to seek out quiet places and solitude in an effort to capture this illusive feeling. I attempted to control my outer life in order to find inner peace. This was successful only on a temporary basis. I had not yet experienced the peacefulness that comes from within—a sensation that emanates from the very core of my being.

Today I know that my sense of peace can be influenced by, but is not dependent on, my external environment. Peace is more than the absence of sounds and people. It is a state of being present to and accepting of myself—of being connected to my feelings and my truth. As I am able to acknowledge, express, and release distressing and disturbing thoughts and feelings—especially those that I have absorbed from others—I will create space within for peace to take root. I will slowly begin to feel glimmers of the inner peace that has eluded me for years.

Distractions and stresses are a reality of life. I may still need to find a quiet place or surround myself with comforting sights and sounds to initially calm my mind and spirit. As I move through my process, I will more easily connect to my growing sense of inner peace. I will know that it is always available to me— sometimes just a breath away. Today I know that I am most deserving of feeling the peace I have longed for and am willing to do whatever it takes to effect this.

❀ This day I affirm that I deserve to at last feel
a true sense of peace. I have lived with chaos
long enough. Whenever I feel disquieted, I
will strive to return to my inner sanctuary of
serenity. I now know the way.

I Can Distance Myself from Non-Supportive Family Members

Perhaps one of the most devastating blows I will have to sustain as a sexual abuse survivor is to experience disbelief, abandonment, accusations, or worse from my family. This is particularly confusing and painful if my abusers were members of my immediate or extended family.

As a child, one of the beliefs I may have clung to was that at least in my home, surrounded by my family, I was safe. To acknowledge betrayal by any of these people was unthinkable. I learned to be loyal even to those who were abusing me. My life and sanity depended on it.

Today, my child-within needs and deserves to be believed, heard, and supported as she walks her very difficult and painful path through recovery. She deserves to know the truth about her family and may need gentle and understanding support as she embraces this reality.

If I need to distance myself from family members to protect my little one and my recovery, I will find the strength to do so. I will own all my feelings about having to do this and will express them with safe people.

Grieving the loss of a family can be excruciating

and continuing to maintain my distance will be challenging. The natural response of my child-within will be to crave her family—especially her parents. When these feelings arise, I will listen to her, comfort her, and protect her. My adult self can provide the strength and stamina to walk with her through her loneliness and sorrow. She and I will heal together.

❀ When my family is non-supportive of my
healing process, I will be there for my child-
within. I will affirm that these people are
missing out on knowing a very precious and
courageous being, and I will tell her so.

I Cherish and Reclaim My Sense of Wonder

As a child, I had a vibrant, natural curiosity about myself and the world around me. I may have wondered about a great many things, perhaps even asking questions of the adults in my life. Sometimes I was rewarded by finding someone who could understand and listen to my innocent, childlike wonderings. These people were truly gifts to my young spirit. More often I was told to stop daydreaming or not to ask so many questions, and so I learned to keep my wonderings to myself. I was learning very early on to hide my natural, spontaneous self in exchange for what I thought was love, guidance, and protection.

When the sexual abuse began to occur, my sense of wonder began to be tainted and tested. I no longer felt as strong a desire to connect to my world as it was becoming unsafe and frightening. I still had many questions but was now afraid to ask the important ones—the ones that were causing me fear, pain, and confusion. And so I adjusted to the questions without answers and the horrific events that could not be understood, while continuing to wonder—albeit in a more subdued and secretive manner.

As my wounded spirit begins to heal, I may be aware of the gradual return of a primal sense of wonder. There will be moments when I am suddenly filled with a sense of awe at the creation of the universe. This is the awakening of the natural sense of wonder that my child-within has guarded so lovingly all these years. I can cherish and relish all the feelings connected to recovering this long-dormant part of me. I will revel in the beauty of my spirit and my world. I will feel my aliveness and wonder to my heart's content. And in my wonderings, I will find myself again.

✿ Today I will be aware of any wondering that I do about myself or my world—and affirm this as a vital and precious part of me. I will ask all the questions that have waited so long to be heard and know that it is safe to do this.

I Am Learning to Respect and Care for My Body

As a sexual abuse survivor, I may have spent most of my life denying that I even had a body. I could see that I had one if I chanced to look in the mirror, but even then it seemed like an illusion. I just couldn't integrate my inside with my outside.

Or I may have gone to the other extreme at times—thinking obsessively about how I looked. Always concerned about my outer appearance and never feeling satisfied with what I saw or perceived was there. I may have abused my body with drugs, diets, bingeing, purging, poor nutrition, extremes in hygiene, overwork, lack of or excessive exercise, or ignoring health needs. In any event, I was not caring for my body in a loving and respectful way.

Today, as I own my sexual abuse and understand how I simply continued the cycle of mistreatment and disrespect my body had already experienced, I can break that cycle by making new, healthy choices. I can begin to take ownership of my body and treat it lovingly. I can learn about healthful nutrition and exercise and practice these principles each day. I can give my body special treats such as warm baths, safe massages, a specially prepared meal, sleep or rest when needed, or a walk in a favorite place. I can love and care for my body because it is a part of me and I am worth it.

❀ My child's body was a precious entity and so is the body of my adult. I will no longer mistreat my body as my abusers did. Instead, I will reclaim it by learning to care for it in loving and affirming ways.

I Can Say That I Need Time to Think about Something Before Answering

I often give people answers long before I feel ready—simply because they ask. I may find that I am particularly susceptible to people who try to hurry me into giving them an answer or decision. I may find myself feeling a great deal of anxiety and ambivalence when given a deadline. Deadlines are useful in that they set limits. They become counterproductive when I turn over my personal power in an attempt to meet them.

It will be important to remember that today I *always* have choices. This was not true for me as a child. The sexual abuse occurred whether or not I consented. I was truly choiceless and powerless.

Having this history of victimization, I often forget that I can take my time before answering. Today I can tell people that I'll get back to them or that I need some time to consider their question or request before answering. In this way, I can minimize "snap" decisions that I may question or obsess about later. In taking my time, I will be affirming my thinking skills, my belief in my inner knowledge, and my adult power.

❀ Today I reclaim my power by verbalizing my need for time to think about decisions. Today I have that freedom of choice that I lacked as a child and will exercise it whenever I can.

111

All My Longings Have Worth

I may often find myself longing for something with an intensity, perhaps even a sense of urgency. This is because there have been so many things that have been absent from my life for so long. As a survivor of sexual abuse, I lacked a loving, nurturing childhood. Many of my childhood dreams and wants have gone unfulfilled. By now, I may have even convinced myself that I did not deserve or was not "meant" to experience the joyous and natural experiences of life.

Although I cannot change the past, I can begin to give credence and recognition to all of my longings today. Some of these longings may be holdovers from my childhood or young adulthood. This is to be expected. I have buried some of my yearnings for so long that they will need special attention to move into my consciousness. Then, and only then, will I be able to experience and move through all my feelings about them.

Longing is something I feel in my heart and often in every cell of my body. It is not something that can be described by mere words. Rather it is a heartfelt desire that I have nurtured into being. Today I acknowledge that I deserve to have all my longings and yearnings. I no longer have to bury them or pretend they don't exist. The important thing is that I allow myself to have them. In this way, I will be experiencing a wholeness of being and the freedom to hope and dream.

❀ Today I accept all of my longings as real, significant, and worthy of my attention.

Today I Accept Where I Am in My Journey

I have always balked at the word *acceptance*. I thought it meant submission to something or someone, and I was not about to submit to anything or anyone! I had already experienced enough of that in my life. As I have engaged in the healing process, I have learned a new definition of acceptance. Today it simply means that I acknowledge reality rather than fighting and flailing against it.

My journey consists of every moment I have lived thus far. Accepting where I have been and where I am in the present, simply means acknowledging what is. Some days this may occur easily. Other days, I may find myself frantically resisting it. These are the times when my life or sanity may seem "on the line." I am overwhelmed by past and present feelings, thoughts, and experiences and feel most vulnerable.

If I can affirm that wherever I am on my journey is OK, then acceptance can begin to ease my inner turmoil. I can learn that acceptance no longer means submission. It simply means embracing myself and life exactly where it is—not where *I* want or think it should be. Today acceptance can have a gentler, more nurturing meaning to me.

❀ **Wherever I am in my journey is perfect and has gifts for me. Today I affirm that I am exactly where I need to be and I am OK.**

I Can Empower Myself

Feeling powerless is something I have experienced repeatedly throughout my life. It began with my first experience of abuse or neglect and has continued into my adulthood. As a child, I became well schooled in learning to react out of a victim stance and found that my offenders encouraged this behavior.

Early disempowerment by my offenders is evident today in my reactions to situations in which I feel unable to protect myself or in which I need to give up some control. I may feel disproportionately angry or fearful or may "freeze" when I find myself in either of these situations. I may fall back into my survivor mode of "politeness" and silence when what I really want to do is to say what I need or confront an offender's shameless behavior head-on.

I can empower myself today by remembering that I am an adult who has a multitude of choices. Affirming these choices will allow me to take actions that are in my best interests and that keep me safe. In instances where I still react as a victim, I will be gentle with myself and think about ways that I can act differently in the future. It will be important to talk to and comfort my child-within as I walk through each situation in which I feel powerless. She needs to know that today someone is here for her and that someone is *me!*

Most empowering will be my willingness to own my powerlessness as I can then see my choices more clearly and act more rationally. I am entitled to my righteous anger and can use this feeling to power me into taking healthy action today.

✿ Today I affirm my ability to reclaim my power and use it to live as a thriver rather than as a victim. I will recognize one instance today in which I empowered myself and celebrate this victory.

I Can Recognize and Affirm My Successes

How often have I heard myself or other survivors say that they can never seem to identify personal successes, much less feel or enjoy them? To feel defeated, at fault, and never enough are *much* more familiar to me. I have been conditioned by my abuse to carry the shame of my offenders, and in that shame there is no room for feeling successful. One of my life patterns may have been to do more and be better in a frantic effort to at last experience those elusive feelings of success and being enough.

In recovery, I may be surprised to discover that I

am beginning to experience fleeting thoughts and feelings of success. From deep within me, I may spontaneously feel a true sense of my own worth and creativity. When I am in a safe place with safe people, I can be an open channel for the truth to move through me. I can at last release the lies and shame that do not belong to me and begin to embrace the real me.

Today I can begin to recognize and affirm my successes even if I do not yet feel or believe in them. I can allow others to identify and affirm my successes while I am learning to do this for myself. I can begin by acknowledging that I am enough and affirm that I am entitled to enjoy all my successes. I will no longer allow my offenders to rob me of what I rightfully deserve. I will especially affirm my greatest success—that of surviving and healing.

My child-within may feel grief and perhaps anger about all her unsung successes. I will help her heal by allowing her to express her feelings and identify all her precious successes that she was not able to enjoy. I will celebrate and enjoy these with her today.

❀ This day, I nurture the belief that I can experience and enjoy my successes—past and present.

I Can Quiet My Obsessive Thinking by Asking My Child-Within What She Needs

Thinking obsessively is second nature to me. I may often find myself "stuck" on one thought or problem. Sometimes it seems that no matter how I try to interrupt these thoughts, they continue and perhaps even escalate in intensity. It can feel maddening not to be able to change my focus. I may feel imprisoned by my own mind.

Often my obsessive thinking is a direct result of some feeling I am not acknowledging or expressing. As a child, this type of thinking was one of the tools I used to prevent myself from knowing what was really happening. If I could focus my thoughts elsewhere, I would not have to feel or think about the sexual abuse. Somehow, this process created an illusion of safety for me.

Today I may experience obsessive thinking in the form of extreme perfectionism or an inability to let go of circumstances beyond my control. I may replay scenarios in my thoughts in hopes that I can somehow change them and therefore change what has already happened. This is the magical thinking of my child-within. She is still trying to change the past so that she won't have to feel the pain and betrayal of the sexual abuse.

I have found that an antidote for my obsessive thinking can be as simple as asking my child-within what she needs. No matter what I am thinking about, it is usually a result of some unresolved feeling. If I take time to consult my child-within, she will have the answer. Once I know what she needs and endeavor to give that to her, I will usually find that my thinking clears.

❀ When I find myself thinking obsessively, I will pause and ask my child-within what she needs. In doing this, I will be placing the focus where it belongs—on her and her many unmet needs and unexpressed feelings.

I Am Learning to Foster a Sense of Gratitude

For most of my life, I have found it quite difficult and almost impossible at times to feel anything akin to gratitude. What, after all, was there to feel grateful for? Being sexually abused as a child had created many feelings and thoughts inside me but gratitude was most likely not one of them. There were times when I couldn't even feel grateful to be alive.

As a survivor, an "attitude of gratitude" will probably not come naturally to me at first. It will be something I will need to consciously foster and nurture. It may begin with feeling thankful for tangible things that I have, such as a place to live, enough food to eat, and clothes to wear. I can then begin to extend it to include some intangibles, such as friends who love and respect me, a sunny day, my ability to think clearly and see options, momentary feelings of joy in being alive, time to do things I enjoy, support of other survivors, or the ability to see and appreciate the preciousness of both my adult and my child-within.

I will never feel grateful for my history of abuse but I can begin to feel grateful that I can heal and truly enjoy my life. I deserve this most assuredly! As I begin to heal and come to terms with my past, I will find that gratitude will begin to occur spontaneously. It is a by-product of my inner joy in being me and the healing of my spiritual woundedness. When I feel most desperate and hopeless, focusing on gratitude can help me return to a state of stability and hope. Even in the darkest situation I can find a small ray of light.

❀ Today I will identify one thing that I can feel truly grateful for in my life and allow myself to experience this feeling of gratitude for as long as I can.

Today I Embrace My Talents

Whenever someone compliments me or acknowledges one of my talents, I may find myself wanting to discount the comment. I may feel anger, shame, pain, or fear. I need to accept that all of these reactions are normal and OK, given my history of abuse.

As a child, my caregivers were not able to see my talents and may have done their best to squelch any recognition of my positive attributes. This is how my abusers were able to ensure that I felt less than and that I would continue to carry their sexual shame. I was indeed a prisoner in my own mind and body.

Today I can see and appreciate that by being willing to walk through my feelings and return those

that are not mine to their rightful owners, I can begin
to reclaim all of my natural talents. I deserve to feel
gratitude and pride for what I was born with,
naturally. I can embrace all that is uniquely me.
This may be a slow process, and I will be patient
with myself, knowing that there will be grieving
before the joy and acceptance can be felt.

❀ Today I take time to acknowledge one of
my talents—even if I cannot yet embrace it
freely. I can trust that I am involved in a
gradual healing process as I reclaim my
authentic self.

Today I Give Credence to All My Feelings

I may be amazed and perhaps even overwhelmed by the range of feelings I have begun to experience in recovery. Not only am I aware of the vast array of feelings I possess, but also the levels of intensity that they can reach—often without warning. I may find that anger quickly develops into rage or that fear becomes terror. I believe that the intensification is a result of the tight containment and denial of feelings I experienced during my years of abuse and neglect.

The "norm" for a sexual abuse survivor is to initially deny, minimize, or rationalize away *any*

feelings that occur. The abuse itself demanded that
I deny as many feelings as possible and that I only
express the ones deemed "acceptable" by my abuser
and caregivers. I learned quickly which of my feelings
would be ignored, discounted, or met with negative
consequences. These are the ones that have been in
my inner "holding tank" for years.

As I am able to *freely* express my feelings, I
may notice that any thoughts of violence, terror, or
self-destructiveness will gradually dissipate. I will
endeavor to acknowledge my feelings as they arise
and express them in ways that are life-supporting. I

may still experience strong injunctions against owning certain feelings, but I can walk through the
discomfort, thus dismantling the restraints and lies
of my abusers.

Today I acknowledge my feelings as an integral
part of my wholeness of being. I no longer need to
shame, deny, or talk myself out of having my feelings.
I can affirm to myself and particularly to my child-
within that all my feelings are acceptable and normal
and deserve to be heard and believed.

❀ Today I give credence to all of my feelings
and recognize their crucial contribution to
my recovery.

I Can Grow from Experiences That Trigger Memories and Feelings

By now I have a well-stocked storehouse of "frozen" feelings and memories that span perhaps decades of my life. The numbing process began as a result of my abuse and probably continued long after the abuse ended. What was once a survival tool became a way of life for me. I became truly adept at burying or freezing any unpleasant feelings—especially those connected to current abusive or victimizing experiences. I skillfully, and probably unconsciously, avoided triggering any feelings or memories from that vast tundra that lay deep inside of me.

My recovery process may have been initiated by an occurrence that triggered a recollection or feeling from the past. Somehow a leak had developed in my well-secured deep freeze and I began to experience feelings and memories that seemed overwhelming and even overreactive for my present circumstances. I was most uncomfortable and confused and may have felt that I was going crazy. I was really just beginning to reclaim my sanity.

Today I may find that special days, changes, sounds, smells, or even the most unexpected stimuli can trigger intense thinking and feeling memories for

me. If I can accept and flow with the experience, I
will discover that the source is some need, thought,
feeling, or incident that I buried long ago. Even
though the experience may seem overwhelming and
permanent, it *will* pass. Each time that I am willing to
embrace whatever is triggered and move through it,
I will be giving myself the gifts of growth and healing.
By confronting the past, I can release it and make
room for new, more nurturing memories.

❀ Today I will strive to see triggers in a positive light. They no longer need to be my enemies. Instead, I can see them as allies offering me opportunities to be released from the bondage of my past. I will discover that I *can* survive and even learn from them. I can use these experiences to help me reclaim yet another precious part of my authentic self.

I Can Relax and Let Go

E ven in recovery, there are and will be days when nothing seems to go right. Feelings and events combine to create what I might label a "terrible day." Chances are that on those days I am experiencing difficulty in relaxing with the flow of life and letting go of outcomes. I have somehow become entrenched once again in old survivor thought and behavior patterns that demand I attempt to be in control. Controlling was a natural response to the terrifying loss of control I felt during my abuse, and it quickly became an integral part of my living style. It is completely understandable, then, that I will continue to revert back to this familiar and "safe" way of being on a regular basis.

Relaxing and letting go, on the other hand, will probably feel completely foreign and unsafe to me. To relax and let go means that I'll have to trust something outside of myself. Trust that I'll be taken care of. That I'll be safe. This new way of approaching life will take a *lot* of practice and patience. I can begin by letting go of small outcomes like whether I receive mail today or how long it will take to reach a particular destination. I can eventually move on to more challenging situations like letting go of something

I've lost, the outcome of a job interview, a relationship that needs to end, or how my plans will turn out.

As I continue to let go, I will find that my life
will become easier, less tense, and more fun. I will
gain a new freedom and will finally feel able to truly
relax. Where "forced" methods of relaxation have
failed in the past, I will find that letting go is the true
path to a sense of well-being and ease of life. There
are days when it's good to know that I'm not, after all,
in charge of the universe. I only need to do what I can
and trust the results to a source greater than myself.

❀ Today I will trust enough to let go of just one thing. I will affirm myself as I do this and celebrate my triumph over the hypervigilant conditioning of the abuse. Today I reclaim my right to relax and enjoy my life.

My Life Is in Process

Waiting is something I am very accustomed to. As a child, it seemed I was always waiting for something—the end of the sexual abuse, the opportunity to leave an abhorrent home life, someone to love me in a healthy way, or to simply be noticed. As I grew older, I may have incorporated this learned mode of waiting into some of my adult desires and dreams. I *expected* to wait for good things to happen in my life. It was the only way I knew to defend against the feelings of hopelessness caused by my abuse.

I may unknowingly be playing out this waiting game in my recovery process today. There are so many wounded parts of me that I may believe I have to place my life "on hold" until I am completely healed. I may be shelving relationships, career goals, and even happiness until I am "fixed." This is a mistaken belief that my child-within still clings to. Today I can affirm that she no longer has to be perfect to get what she deserves. She no longer has to wait to live a full and joyous life.

Today I can recognize and acknowledge the parts of me that need healing and honor any limitations I may have in these areas. As I heal, I can keep myself safe *and* take risks so that I am always in the flow of life. Today I can be a participant in life, not just an observer who is waiting for her turn.

❀ **This day I allow myself to be in midstream rather than waiting on the banks. My life is happening now. It is up to me to live it.**

There Is Always Hope

To be hopeful is to believe that positive change can take place. This attitude can seem virtually impossible to adopt when I am in the emotional valleys of life's journey. I may have vague memories of times when I did feel hopeful, but these seem out of reach and even unreliable during my periods of deepest despair. Rather, a posture of hope*less*ness is one with which I am more familiar and "comfortable." It was created by my abuse and has defined my beliefs about my life for many years.

Hope and despair cannot coexist. When I am feeling most cynical about the existence of hope in my life, I will need to truly be on a walk of faith. There is a life spark within me searching fervently for even a flutter of a breeze. I can supply this needed element by being willing to listen to other survivors who are feeling and expressing hope and know that it exists for me too. Hope *will* return, even though I cannot believe it. It will be miraculous. It may not come right away, but it will come. All I need to do is hang on until that moment arrives. I will not see it coming. I will not know how it will happen. It just will. And I will wonder how I ever doubted its existence.

I will continue through this cycle of hope and despair as long as I need to during my recovery process. I will endeavor to be accepting and understanding of myself as I move through these necessary stages.

❀ **During my darkest times, I will remind myself that the light of hope is resting in the very core of my being, waiting patiently to emerge once again.**

Helpful Resources

Books

Adams, Christine A. *One-Day-At-A-Time Therapy*. St. Meinrad, IN: St. Meinrad Archabbey, 1990.

Anonymous ACOA. *This New Day*. Delaware Water Gap, PA: Quotidian Publishers, 1988.

Bass, Ellen, and Laura Davis. *The Courage to Heal*. New York: Harper & Row, 1988.

Beattie, Melody. *Beyond Co-Dependence*. San Francisco: Harper & Row, 1989.

——. *The Language of Letting Go*. San Francisco: HarperCollins, 1990.

Berkus, Rusty. *Appearances*. Encino, CA: Red Rose Press, 1984.

——. *To Heal Again*. Encino, CA: Red Rose Press, 1986.

Black, Claudia. *It's Never Too Late to Have a Happy Childhood*. New York: Ballantine Books, 1989.

Blume, E. Sue. *Secret Survivors*. New York: John Wiley and Sons, 1990.

Bozarth-Campbell, Alla. *Life Is Goodbye, Life Is Hello*. Minneapolis, MN: Compcare, 1982.

Brady, Maureen. *Daybreak*. San Francisco: HarperCollins, 1991.

Covington, Stephanie. *Awakening Your Sexuality*. San Francisco: HarperCollins, 1991.

Daugherty, Lynn B. *Why Me?* Racine, WI: Mother Courage Press, 1984.

Davis, Laura. *The Courage to Heal Workbook*. New York: Harper & Row, 1990.

———. *Allies in Healing*. New York: HarperCollins, 1991.

Dean, Amy. *Night Light*. Minneapolis: Hazelden, 1986.

Edens, Cooper. *The Art of Longing*. San Marcos, CA: Green Tiger Press, 1986.

Fahy, Mary. *The Tree That Survived the Winter*. Mahwah, NJ: Paulist Press, 1989.

Fishel, Ruth. *Time for Joy*. Deerfield Beach, FL: Health Communications Inc., 1988.

Forward, Dr. Susan, with Craig Buck. *Toxic Parents*. New York: Bantam Books, 1989.

Gil, Eliana. *Outgrowing the Pain*. New York: Dell, 1983.

Hartman, Cherry. *Be-Good-to-Yourself Therapy*. St. Meinrad, IN: Abbey Press, 1987.

Haury, Don. *I'm Not My Fault*. Scottsdale, AZ: Safe Place Publishers, 1990.

Lew, Mike. *Victims No Longer*. New York: Harper & Row, 1990.

Love, Dr. Patricia. *The Emotional Incest Syndrome*. New York: Bantam Books, 1990.

Maltz, Wendy, and Beverly Holman. *Incest and Sexuality*. Washington, DC: Lexington Books, 1987.

Mellody, Pia, with Andrea Wells Miller and J. Keith Miller. *Facing Co-Dependence*. San Francisco: Harper & Row, 1989.

Middleton-Moz, Jane and Lorie Dwinell. *After the Tears*. Pompano Beach, FL: Health Communications, 1986.

Miller, Alice. *Banished Knowledge*. New York: Doubleday, 1990.

Thomas, T. *Surviving With Serenity*. Deerfield Beach, FL: Health Communications, Inc., 1990.

W. Nancy. *On the Path*. San Francisco: HarperCollins, 1991.

Pamphlets

Caruso, Beverly. *The Impact of Incest*. Center City, MN: Hazelden, 1987.

Kunzman, Kristin A. *Healing from Childhood Sexual Abuse*. Center City, MN: Hazelden, 1989.

Tapes

Baldwin, Martha. *Change of Heart*. Oklahoma City, OK: Rainbow Books, 1989.

Beattie, Melody. *Language of Letting Go*. Plymouth, MN: Metacom Inc., Hazelden, 1990.

Fisher, Amy. *Healing the Spiritual Wound*. San Diego, CA: Listen to Learn Tapes, Recovery Resources, 1988.

Mellody, Pia. *Co-Dependency Recovery, Spirituality, and Self-Care*. Wickenburg, AZ: Listen to Learn Tapes, Recovery Resources, 1988.

————. *Permission to Be Precious*. Wickenburg, AZ: Listen to Learn Tapes, Recovery Resources, 1987.

Support Groups

Incest Survivors Anonymous (ISA)
P.O. Box 5613
Long Beach, CA 90805-0613

Survivors of Incest Anonymous (SIA)
P.O. Box 21817
Baltimore, MD 21222-6817

My Personal Index

The index can be used to further personalize this book. It may be helpful to write down feelings or associations that come to mind when reading certain affirmations or to note which affirmation was helpful to you in a certain situation. For example, the affirmation "There Is Always Hope" may have been especially comforting and uplifting at a time when you felt discouraged. You may want to write this down so that the next time you are confronted with this feeling, you can refer back to the affirmation that was of help.

Topic/situation   **Page**

_____

_____

_____

_____

_____

Topic/situation   **Page**

_____

_____

_____

_____

_____

_____

_____

_____

_____

_____

_____

_____

_____

_____

_____

_____

_____

Topic/situation   **Page**

Topic/situation   **Page**

_____

_____

_____

_____

_____

_____

_____

_____

_____

_____

_____

_____

_____

_____

_____

_____

_____

Topic/situation   **Page**

_____

_____

_____

_____

_____

_____

_____

_____

_____

_____

_____

_____

_____

_____

_____

_____

_____

Notes

_____

_____

_____

_____

_____

_____

_____

_____

_____

_____

_____

_____

_____

_____

_____

_____